THE AUTOBIOGRAPHY OF THE

REV. WILLIAM STEVENSON

THE AUTOBIOGRAPHY OF THE

REV. WILLIAM STEVENSON

EDITED BY TED A. CAMPBELL

Bridwell Press
Southern Methodist University
Dallas, Texas

Bridwell Press is the professional
publishing arm of Bridwell Library
(SMU Libraries and Perkins School of Theology).
Southern Methodist University

SMU Libraries SMU Perkins School of Theology

Design by Alicia Beebe

Printed in the United States of America

ISBN: 978-1-957946-19-1 (paperback)
ISBN: 978-1-957946-20-7 (open access)

Cover image: "Going to Conference." Published in Eggleston, Edward. *Circuit Rider: A Tale of a Heroic Age.* New York: J. B. Ford & Co., 1874. This print represents a nineteenth century circuit-riding preacher on horseback. No images of William Stevenson are known to exist. Bridwell Library Special Collections, SMU.

CONTENTS

FOREWORD

A decade ago my colleague Dr. Ted Campbell, Albert C. Outler Professor of Wesley Studies, undertook the task of bringing the present volume before a greater audience. *The Autobiography of the Rev. William Stevenson* had lain dormant for the better part of a century and a half, with a brief reemergence in the 1930s, when a typescript version of *The Autobiography* was sent to SMU and eventually ended up in the Bridwell Library archives. When the opportunity arose to publish this historically significant work in the 21st century, Bridwell Library staff rose to the occasion and made that happen in 2015. For decades, Bridwell had published high quality monographs mostly related to exhibitions and collections. In the 1970s, Bridwell even published the biography of a ballet dancer called *Danse Macabre: The Life and Death of Andreas Pavley* by Arthur Corey. In the last few years, with the establishment of the library's professional publishing operation Bridwell Press, it was a natural fit to consider the Stevenson work from a decade ago for republication under our new operations. The present edition allows for a broader readership with our freely available e-book option and will be a valuable contribution to our Methodist publications series at the Bridwell Press. We hope that readers will find this and other works informative, interesting, and useful, and we look forward to presenting more quality historical writings in the years to come.

Anthony J. Elia
J.S. Bridwell Foundation Endowed Librarian and Director, Bridwell Library & Associate Dean of Special Collections and Academic Publishing

EDITOR'S INTRODUCTION

William Stevenson (1768-1857) was a pioneer itinerant Methodist preacher in the southwestern United States. In 1814 or 1815, probably 1815,[1] he became the first Protestant of any denomination to preach within the bounds of what is today Texas. He was also among the first Methodists or Protestants to preach in Arkansas and Oklahoma as well.[2] Stevenson's *Autobiography* given here is a classic account of frontier and folk Methodism, although it has never been published in its entirety since it first appeared in serial form in the *New Orleans Christian Advocate* in the year after Stevenson died.[3]

The *Autobiography* of William Stevenson illustrates many of the distinctive characteristics of Methodist life in the period it covers. Stevenson was ordained as a deacon by none other than Francis Asbury and William McKendree (see heading 1809 below). His narrative depicts him passing through the recognizable stages of Christian experience as Methodists typically described a Christian's "way of salvation," including prolonged struggles of the soul before conversion (see headings 1768-1786, circa 1789, 1792, and 1792-1798), the experience of conversion accompanied by the assurance of pardon (heading 1800a), and his own experience of entire sanctification (heading circa 1801). He described conviction and conversion on the part of others, such as the conversions of his wife and his daughter Elizabeth (heading circa 1802).[4] He defended Methodist beliefs about the universal availability of salvation against Presbyterians (headings 1768-1786 and 1792), and he defended the Methodist practice of infant baptism against Baptists (heading circa 1800b). Stevenson asserted the importance of the means of grace even before one's conversion (heading 1792-1798),[5] and he could quote Charles Wesley verses, apparently from memory (see the four lines quoted under heading 1813).

William Stevenson's *Autobiography* also illustrates broader currents of American Protestant life in this age. He described the phenomenon of "the jerks" associated with highly emotional revivalism in the Second Great Awakening, and he offered accounts of miraculous healings associated with fervent prayer (both described under heading circa 1802). He seems to have had the sense, common to folk religious undercurrents, that almost every event, almost every feeling he had, resulted somehow from the leading of divine grace (heading circa 1788).

William Stevenson's *Autobiography* also illustrates the general history of the American southwest in the period immediately after the Louisiana Purchase.

Although he was not quite the first Methodist preacher to cross the Mississippi, he was in Missouri by 1807 (heading 1807), and he gives a rich account of the settlement of Arkansas (heading 1813 and following). He was an eyewitness to the devastating New Madrid earthquakes that occurred between 1811 and 1812 (heading 1811-1812), and he noted his preaching in "the province of Texas" in 1815, when it was still part of the Viceroyalty of New Spain (heading 1814-1815).

The last year that Stevenson described in his *Autobiography* was 1816. He stated toward the end of the work that he was in his seventy-third year of life when he wrote it. That would place the composition of his *Autobiography* around 1841, and in fact he mentioned the year 1841 as contemporary with his writing of it (see under heading 1813). The work was not published, however, until fourteen years later, in the year after Stevenson died.

The Autobiography of the Rev. William Stevenson was published serially in *The New Orleans Christian Advocate* between March 13 and April 24, 1858, as noted in the chapter titles given below. The editor of this denominational newspaper at that time was Dr.

Holland N. McTyeire, later a bishop of the Methodist Episcopal Church, South, who was also instrumental in the founding of Vanderbilt University. A typescript of the *Autobiography* was sent to SMU in 1936 at the request of SMU President C. C. Selecman, and the present text has been made from this typescript copy in Bridwell Library and subsequently checked against the original publication in the *New Orleans Christian Advocate*, which has been made available online by the Louisiana Annual Conference Archives Center at Centenary College.

One of the characteristics of this work is to utilize extremely long paragraphs. For the sake of contemporary readers, I have broken some of these into shorter paragraphs, noting my added paragraph breaks with this symbol: [¶]. I have also added headings within each chapter indicating the chronology of the *Autobiography* to give a means of locating passages within the text. Otherwise the text is given as it appears in the original publication in the *New Orleans Christian Advocate*, preserving the spelling and punctuation that appear there.

I want to thank the staff of Bridwell Library for their efforts in publishing this *Autobiography*, including library Director Roberta Schaafsma and Archivist Timothy Binkley, who undertook the layout of the work. I am also indebted to several students who volunteered to assist in the work of proof reading this manuscript, checking it against the original publication, and I want to express my gratitude to Carrie Leader, David Rivera, José Sanchez-Perry, Evan Jones, and Amanda Bresciani.

Ted A. Campbell
Professor of Church History Perkins School of Theology
Southern Methodist University Dallas, Texas
1 June 2015

INTRODUCTORY COMMENT

By Holland N. Mctyeire,

Editor of *The New Orleans Christian Advocate*

Under this head, we purpose furnishing our readers several numbers on experimental and practical religion, readable and edifying. The autobiography of Rev. Wm. Stevenson was furnished by Rev. J. Pipes. He [Stevenson] died last year in Bastrop[6] Parish, La. – died a hopeful, happy Christian death. He had been for more than forty years a preacher of the gospel, and was the pioneer who planted the Church in Southern Arkansas and North Louisiana. Let such be had in honor. There is a lesson in such a life.

Ed.

From *The New Orleans Christian Advocate*

MARCH 13, 1858

[1768-1786]

I was born in South Carolina on the 4th of October, 1768, near a station called Ninety-Six[7], a frontier not far from the Cherokee line. My parents were brought up in, and belonged to the Presbyterian Church, and I was baptized when an infant by a minister of that order, and brought up in the fear of God. When I was five years old, my mother became uneasy about the salvation of her soul, sought and found peace with God, through faith in our Lord Jesus Christ, and joined the Baptist Church. Some of them were warm hearted, shouting Christians, and my mother obtained like precious faith. That class then were looked upon by the old, calm, still-born regulars[8], as a kind of weak, enthusiastic brethren, but good Christians, and should be borne with in the Church.

Among these kind of people I was raised. I frequently heard the Presbyterians preach; but never heard a Methodist until I was twenty years of age. God made my mother a peculiar blessing to me; I had no doubt of her religion. Her faith was a living faith, producing holiness of life. From her walk and conversation I received correct ideas of true religion, which fastened deep and lasting conviction on my heart, before I was eight years of age. I viewed the great God as the creator and preserver of all things in heaven and earth, and from what my mother told me about Him. I believed He was holy, just and good, and that His mercy was over all His works,[9] and that He was not willing that any should perish,[10] but that all men had power given them from him to repent and believe in Jesus Christ and live.

I frequently heard, in my raising, much said in favor of the doctrine of decrees, unconditional election and reprobation; but I never could believe that a God, just and merciful, would ever will, much less decree such great abominations, and even in my boyhood, before I was ten years of age, I seriously doubted any man who said he believed that doctrine; for I then viewed it as blasphemy.[11] No, no, no, thought I; God is too good to do the devil's work for him. Will God furnish the materials, do all the work, find himself, and give the devil half? He owes the devil nothing, and will not work for him to keep him peaceable. Always, when I sinned, I condemned myself, and not God, in any sense. I felt that it would be just in Him to send me to hell for my own faults, for my own sins, which I ungodly had committed. And that God was worthy to be loved and praised for his goodness and mercy, in sparing such a wretch.

Thus I lived many years, sinning and repenting; making solemn covenants to lead a new life, to seek the conversion of my soul; for I believed that I must be converted, I must be born again or lost forever. I often cried to God for mercy, and would for awhile forsake the company of bad young men; but again fall a prey to the snares and follies of youth, except those base crimes called scandalous, such as stealing, perjury, willful lying, or deceiving the weaker vessels[12] in breaking a marriage promise. In my young days, I therefore endeavored to avoid such; but I always viewed myself as unprepared for heaven, and I knew by reading the word of God that I had not religion, for all that had it had the witness in themselves.[13]

I believed that regeneration was the work of God's Spirit in the heart, and that the Spirit would always bear witness to his own work. I believed the word of God to be true, and that, if I ever did get converted, I should certainly know it by the witness of the Spirit of God that had done the work in my soul. I had daily the witness of condemnation in my own heart, which made me often cry, "Lord save, or I perish."[14] My life was truly a life of bondage[15] for more than twenty years, knowing my Master's will, but doing it not; while the judgments of God, mixed with mercies, followed me all my days of sin. I will mention a few of them, out of very many, as specimens of God's dealings with me:

[circa 1786]

When about eight years of age[16] a horse ran away with me, and ran under the branch of a tree which brought my head against the side of the tree, and a dead snag, as large as a man's finger and about five or six inches long run into my right eye. I fell to the ground, but the horse ran on. I soon arose to my feet, and putting my hand up found the snag very fast in the socket of my eye, and the eye, what was left, thrust out on my temple. I took fast hold of the snag with my right hand, but I could not move it. I then took hold of it with both hands and brought it out by a quick jerk, like pulling a tooth. I then put my fingers into the socket and pulled out some dead bark and splinters which came off the snag, and pressed my eye back into its place. While in great pain and bleeding freely, I fell on my knees and cried, "Lord, I know if thou wilt, thou canst restore my eye again. Have mercy on me; I will be thine from this time and forever." I then believed God had done this for my disobedience,[17] and felt resolved to disobey him no more. I felt faith that God would have mercy and restore my sight, which was the case, in four months, contrary to the opinions of almost all who saw the wound. Almost all that part of the ball between the sight and my nose was cut away and came out in the healing. The third day, a doctor of great skill, probed it and examined it closely; when my mother asked him if he thought it would ever recover the sight again, he replied, "I do not know, madam; if God please, he will." So thought I; so I think now, that God in mercy did hear my prayer.

[circa 1788]

About two years after, I fell from a ridgepole of a log house. At the raising, I was sitting on a short log, on which the ridgepole was to lie, and while pulling very hard by a rope, in bringing up the ridgepole, the rope broke and the log on which I sat turned over and threw me head foremost. I fell between two of the joists of the upper floor, and on one of the sleepers[18] of the lower; yet was able to rise to my feet and climb over the wall to get out, as there was no other passage. It is true I was hurt; but not materially. I was able to ride home about two miles. I was deeply affected in mind, especially in the act of falling headlong. I then felt that my life certainly was at an end, and had no hope after death, but a certain fearful looking for of that death which never dies. In the midst of these despairing thoughts, another thought, quick as lightning, passed through my mind – that God could save me. I cried to him for help, and strange as it may appear, before I reached the ground, falling amongst the sleepers, I had a little faith, as a grain of mustard seed,[19] that God would save me, and so he did; and from that time to this, I am assured it was a providential interposition. O my soul, love thou the Lord. Love thou the Lord, for thou hast been plucked as a brand from the burning.[20]

Shortly after this I rode ten miles to hear a new kind of a preacher called a Methodist; and as I never had heard one of that order I was desirous to see the man and hear what he had to say. There was a large congregation. Many, like myself, came to hear the stranger. He was a godly looking man, having a solemnity[21] about him which commanded attention; he preached under the trees, in the open air, as the house was too small; his text was, "If a man abide not in me, he is cast forth as a branch and is withered and men gather them into the fire and they are burned."[22] I heard with attention, found no fault with the man or with the doctrines. I viewed myself as a dry branch or as one out of Christ; and of course, I must be burned or converted, and become a faithful branch of Christ, the true vine. As I returned home to my father's house, I rode with a young man, an old friend and companion in sin and folly. He asked me what I thought of the preaching. I said that man was a good preacher. "Yes," said he, "and I thought when he was preaching about those withered, dead branches being gathered and burned, that you and I would be amongst them." I said I hoped not; we must turn and seek religion. "There is no hope for us; I know that we shall both go to hell." I told him God was good and merciful, and if we would turn from all our sins and seek, we should find mercy and be saved.

He said he had no hope at all that he should ever be any better than he was; and that he knew he should go to hell at last, and I was sure to go with him. I was terrified at his conversation, and tried to remove his fear and unbelief; but all in vain. I saw we were both in the broad road[23] – he through despair and I in presumption – two dreadful chains, in which Satan leads his captives. May God help his servants, the preachers, to break them both by pointing out the remedy. [¶]

The same evening, when I returned to home, I met an old uncle, the Rev. James Fowler, a Baptist preacher, a man of eminence in that Church.[24] I was glad to see him, as he was a friend and always showed me kindness. He asked me if I had been to hear a Methodist preach, that day. I had. Well, where was his text? The gospel of St. John, 15th chapter 6th verse. I repeated the text. How did he preach on that text? I told him as well as I could. He said that was a strange thing to him, that, after a man was made a living branch in Christ he could wither, be cut off and be burned. But, said he, all the Methodists hold that doctrine.[25] His observations on that text surprised me much, as I believed him to be a man of strong mind and well read; for I could not see what other doctrine could, with any degree of consistency, be advanced from the text, taking it in connection with the context and the whole chapter, which is exceedingly plain. I thought much, and more and more, of the great danger of prejudice, prepossession, and of preferring man's creeds and notions to the plain written word of God. Let creeds be reasonable, scriptural and always leading the minds of men to a holy obedience to God and his law, and no good man will fall out with them; but when they act as opiates to keep us easy in our sins they are of the devil.[26] I think the above preacher's name was Ellis.[27] [¶]

[circa 1789]

The second Methodist preacher I heard was Coleman Carlisle – perhaps a year after.[28] His text was: "How shall we escape if we neglect so great salvation."[29] He was truly a son of thunder.[30] I had heard many preachers, of other orders, before him, and had felt very serious under some of them; but I never had such feelings under preaching as I had that day. He first pointed out the great salvation; secondly, the neglectors of that salvation; thirdly, he showed, in a clear and most terrible light, what the neglectors were not to escape; and while on this last head, it appeared to me that the power of God filled the whole house, which was large and overflowing with men and women. A cry was heard, through the whole house for mercy,[31] except in the gallery, where all the young men had taken seats, where I was also. But, if all felt as I did, it was terrible; for I plainly saw under the last head, just what I believe every sinner will feel, when the trumpet shall sound. This indeed was a nail in a sure place, which never left me altogether.

In secret I often cried, "O wretched man that I am, who shall deliver me from the body of this death."[32] When I would do good evil was present with me. I wanted religion on easy terms; the cross was too heavy, I refused it on God's terms, waited for a more convenient season and thus traveled on for years, a poor wretched condemned sinner; confessing judgment but taking every stay. I read God's word often, in which I plainly saw his ways to man. I saw that he was not willing that any should perish, but that all might repent and live.

I had a great desire to unite with God's people, so that I might live with them. – But I thought it would be one of the greatest sins I could commit, to join the Church without first having religion.[33] This was a great error among the Baptist people where I lived and among whom I was raised; and this doctrine I drank so deeply it was a miracle of God's goodness that I was not ruined for ever; for had I had an opportunity of knowing the people called Methodists and been admitted on trial as a seeker and attended prayer and class meeting, I should have had religion many years before I obtained it.[34] O, what a pity it is to see professors[35] and teachers shutting the door against the seekers and children, the young lambs of the flock for whom Christ died, driving them from the fold to live in the open fields, there to await, out of the pales of the Church and God's appointed means of grace, until they get religion. May God have mercy upon poor little children and seekers that are thus neglected and driven from the fold of Christ, and told that they are not fit to come in until they can give a Christian's experience. – God will require the blood of these souls at their hands. [¶]

I could not be admitted into the Church and there brought up in the fear of God, and of course I must remain out among the wicked, who were to be my only comrades and associates, and who never failed to lead my poor weak soul away from God. When I look back upon my past life, before I found favor with God, I clearly see why it was that I remained out of Christ for so long.

It was for want of help. Had I been admitted to the church and taught, as children should always be, I would doubtless have been a happy, pious youth at least twenty years before I escaped from the snare of the devil. O what a loss I have felt, at twenty years, through false instructions. Thus I was led captive by the devil at his will, through that great and youth-destroying doctrine, that you must not come into Christ's Church until you have a Christian experience, you must not go into the school of Christ until you are a good scholar. The young trees must not be planted in the orchard until they bear good fruit. All such doctrines are destructive in the Church and out of the Church. They bind men, women and children fast in chains and keep them back from their rightful Sovereign and Savior. O, when will the whole Church of God wake up to a just sense of the salvation of their children! Thanks be to God, there is much doing and more will yet be done to save the children as they grow up. O, that parents, preachers and teachers would unite every where to pray, preach, exhort and teach children the way to Jesus their Savior who died for them.

I hope the reader will forgive me for detaining him so long about children and youths, when I tell him I was a child myself and recollect the blessings of some good instructions which led me to God; and the curse of false doctrines, which were only calculated to drive me from him. Thus I lived and grew up to manhood, repenting and sinning, hoping and sometimes almost desponding of ever finding mercy of the Lord. In this condition of mind, I left my father, mother, brothers and sisters, then living in Chester county, S. C., where we had suffered greatly in the revolutionary war. All was peace, but the pressure of the times was great, money very scarce, lands poor, and little encouragement for a young man to begin the world or make a living; but we had fine news from the West. Kentucky and Tennessee were fine countries, land plenty and good: so I set out to explore, settle and get rich.[36]

From *The New Orleans Christian Advocate*

MARCH 20, 1858

[1792]

I left home, in company with a beloved cousin and friend, Stevenson Fowler, a son of the Rev. James Fowler, who gave me some books on doctrines, hoping that I would be saved from those great errors, propagated by Arminians.[37] I took the books with thanks to the good man, promising to read them. We started out into a wide world, made our way across the Blue Ridge, the Iron Mountain and some others.[38] All was new – mountains, beautiful springs, and small rivers, rich valleys, bearing fine crops of corn, The farmers had just commenced gathering the corn, as it was in the fall of the year 1792.[39] We were well pleased in traveling down the rivers, Wataga, and Nalacheekey;[40] the country appeared to us romantic, and we found the people kind. [¶]

We had some relations on Nalacheekey river, in Green county, all having considerable families. We called to see them, get acquainted and rest a few days. We were entire strangers to each other; had been acquainted by writing only. They received us joyfully. This is what is now called East Tennessee,[41] then a new country and bordering upon the Cherokee line, who were then at open war with the settlers of Kentucky and Tennessee; and frequent massacres were committed by the Indians five or six miles from the habitation of my uncle. When a murder was committed, the Indians were pursued and sometimes taken and killed. Thus the whites lived and enjoyed themselves quite well, being fearless of the enemy, keeping themselves armed and ready to avenge the blood of their fellow-citizens any time when called for. [¶]

After we had been here among our friends a few days, they began to press on us to stay among them, as the roads to Cumberland and Kentucky were dangerous, and many were murdered on the way. They wished us to teach school for them, as there could be two very good schools raised about six miles apart. We agreed to do so; the schools were soon made up and we commenced about the same time. I taught an English school five days in the week and a singing school on Saturday.[42] Thus I felt well employed all the time and on the Sabbath we could hear the Rev. Hezekiah Balch preach at his chapel at Greenville.[43]

The first time I went to hear him I paid particular attention to his sermon, hearing that he was a very learned Presbyterian preacher. I sat a little to one side, made some notes on his divisions and doctrines for my own satisfaction. One of his congregation asked me, after meeting, if I was not studying divinity in order to become a preacher, as he saw me making notes? I told him I was not; but did so to get a right knowledge of what I heard, which was the truth, for I had no design of criticizing, but to gain knowledge. This was what I always desired from my youth up, to get good sound knowledge on every subject on which I thought or spoke. I never could take the wrong side of a question in a debate knowingly. I had no particular objections to the Rev. H. Balch or his doctrines in general, as they were practical and led to obedience and virtue; but had some objections to his strong prejudices against other denominations. It is true, he was a predestinarian; but moderate. I also attended Methodist preaching frequently, and thought well of their doctrines, practice and charity. They were willing that all should be saved and come to the knowledge of the truth:[44] this pleased me, for I did wish to be saved; and I thought if God ever passed by one he might pass by me. [¶]

While I was teaching school I thought it my duty to teach the children, every evening after spelling, some important truth which might lead them from vice to virtue. I would ask them about God; what was his will concerning us; what is religion; what is repentance; what is faith; what will be the end of the good people, and also of the wicked? After asking such questions, and hearing their thoughts on them, I would try to explain and make all plain to their minds and them give them some useful questions to be answered by every one the next evening before I gave them my ideas on it. This I think was useful; but strange to think, I myself was in bondage to sin. Also, in my singing school, I felt solemn when singing many beautiful lines; my heart was pained within me. While thus employed I enjoyed myself very well, except dying and going to judgment, which haunted my guilty conscience, as I believe it does all gospel taught sinners. [¶]

[1792-1798]

I lived six years in this settlement in Green county, in which time I married, settled myself and worked hard for the common supports of life, served a term of three months against the Indians, passed through many dangers, once narrowly escaped being drowned in swimming a river; at another time ventured my life to save a drowning man, taking him from the jaws of death, when he was about to sink the third time.[45] I removed to Virginia to please my wife's father and mother, whom I loved as I did my own; only stayed there about three months; made a little money and set out for Kentucky, on the last day of March, 1798. I remained one year in Lexington, Ky., taught school nine months, made a crop of corn, sold out and removed to Shelby county; the place of my spiritual and second birth, of which I will now speak. I made a good crop, the first year, got a good start, and begun to live comfortably, after a long round of troublesome removes. [¶]

Now I began again to think of God's unspeakable goodness to me from my infancy. I had a good companion and three fine, promising children; but while viewing my ungratefulness to God and his goodness to me, I was taken with the fever and in a few days despaired of life, without the hope of future happiness. My case appeared just as it was, a desperate one. I prayed or tried to pray for mercy; but thought it too late. I had broken my covenant so often, God will hear me no more. I though if some of the preachers would come and pray for me perhaps God would hear them. [¶]

While I was thinking of these things, an old Methodist man came in to see me; he asked me how I was. I said bad enough; I believe I shall die. He said what do you think about dying? I said I do not regard death as if I was prepared for it; but I am not. O, that some of the preachers would come and pray for me. He said if you are willing I will pray for you. The old man bowed down and prayed so sincerely for me that I got faith that God would restore me again, and I mended from that moment. I set out to seek the Lord; but the more I prayed the worse I got in my estimation; for I began to see the power and opposition of the carnal mind within, which is enmity against God.[46] I was in bondage to an enemy too strong for me – one bred and born and raised up in my very nature. A strong man kept his goods in safety.[47] I saw the good, and right way. My mind was enlightened by God's word and Spirit. I strove to do good; but evil, the carnal mind, was present;[48] my heart was hard – so hard that it refused to bend or break. [¶]

I attended preaching, reading the word of God and private prayer for months.[49] This was the desire of my heart to be holy, and I strove to get the victory day after day. I knew my enemy was my carnal mind, and I believed that none but God, none but Christ the

Savior could deliver me; but the question in my mind was, Will he save me – will he ever speak and say, "I will, be thou clean?" Doubts arose. I thought perhaps my day of grace was past. What shall I do? The promise came: "Seek and ye shall find."[50] My heart said, Lord I will seek thee while I have breath, and if I perish I perish at thy feet. I had a little hope that God, for Christ's sake, would have mercy upon me; for I saw that by the rules of justice I was damned; and if Jesus Christ did not pay my debt, I was gone. So I cried. "Lord save, or I perish."[51] I tried to believe in the Lord Jesus Christ with my whole heart and mind. [¶]

[1800a]

On the 11th of May, 1800, I set out to a meeting to hear the Rev. Gabriel Woodfield, a Methodist, preach. I went praying on my way, and before I came to the house turned aside to pray, in secret, that God would do something for me that day; and while on my knees I felt a comfortable hope that God would do that work within my heart which I so much desired. I went to the meeting; the congregation was large. The preacher gave out a hymn and we sung together. I felt glad I was there. When we kneeled in prayer, my heart was broke for sorrow to think I had been so ungrateful, to so good a father and preserver as God had always been to me. I wept all the time the preacher was preaching. I had a hope that these good Methodists would pray for me before they left the house; but the people were dismissed; all went away and left me alone pleading with God for mercy and resolving to obey him, as a servant, if I should never be received as a son.[52] I prayed in my family from that time, and began to talk to all my family and friends, praying them to turn to God and go with me to heaven, although I had no witness of my own pardon. I said to all around me, "I will serve God or die a trying." Three weeks passed on in this way with me. Some said I would go crazy. I replied I had better lose my senses than my soul. [¶]

On Sunday, the last day of May, I went to a Baptist meeting. The Rev. Mr. Morris preached rather a cold sermon; yet I was glad to hear any kind of preaching, so it led the mind to God. After preaching he sat down by me, conversed with me on the subject of religion. I was pleased and talked freely. He asked me to tell him the exercise of my mind on the subject of religion, and also what I had experienced. I did so, telling him freely without keeping anything back. When I had ended speaking he asked me if I was willing he should tell me what he thought of me. I said I was, but, before he spoke a word, I retracted and said, no sir, I am not willing you should tell me what you think of me. Why, said he, are you not willing. I replied, a thought run through my mind that you will tell me that I have religion and that my soul was converted, which I think would be dangerous for me; it might settle my soul on a sandy foundation, for I know that I have not the witness of God's spirit in me that I am born again.[53] But I hope I shall yet be made free indeed; I want the witness.[54][¶]

He laughed and said, the devil is very cunning. After a little time I thought I was under a wrong apprehension; perhaps the good man was about to tell me something that might be for my good. I then said, sir, I am willing you should tell me honestly what you think of me. He said if you are willing, I will do so. I am perfectly willing. Well, said he, if ever I had religion in my life you have got it. My experience and yours are the same. My soul was converted some time before I would consent to believe it; but meeting with men of experience, they convinced me that I had religion, and if I would believe it then I would be satisfied.[55] I did believe it and now have been preaching many years and have never gone farther than the hope you have got. You are looking for a miracle, but you will never get it in this life. [¶]

I sat and wept to think, if this be true that I might live all my days on a mere hope that I am converted, and never get the witness, never be made free until death. He then told me my experience was good, and if I would then go with him to the water he would baptise me with the Christian baptism. But I could not consent to receive baptism on my present experience. So I bid him farewell, and returned home, but can not describe the exercise of my troubled and embarrassed mind through that evening and night. [¶]

I had set up prayer in my family three weeks before. On the night after hearing G. Woodfield preach we had family prayer. I thought I would still wait on the Lord, hoping he would do something more for me. The morning being the Sabbath, the first day of June, 1800, I arose early; the birds were singing songs of praise to God. I felt a desire to join them in the solitary grove.[56] I left my family in bed, walked to the grove, where all nature was still and solitary except the little innocent birds. I thought, God will do something for me this morning; I will kneel here and wrestle with him in prayer. I fell on my knees to pray; but the Holy Spirit was beforehand with me, and on me, and in me. Before I made one petition, my intended prayer was turned into praises to Him who had loved me and washed me in his own blood.[57] I had the witness, God's Spirit bearing witness with my spirit that I was a child of God:[58] I experienced the truth of God's word, he that believeth on the Son hath life.[59] God is love, and he that dwelleth in love dwelleth in God and God in him.[60] Old things were passed away – all appeared new.[62] I loved him because he first loved me;[62] I also loved the whole human family. My heart was united in love to the children of God. I loved them as myself, and I loved the unconverted with a love of pity. [¶]

O Lord, I will praise thee for the unspeakable blessing[63] freely given to prepare my unworthy soul for union and communion with the Father, and with his Son, my only Savior Jesus Christ: glory to God. Although forty-two years have gone by since I received that unspeakable blessing, yet I feel the same thing. Glory to God, who is just and justifies all who believe in Jesus Christ.[64] And now being justified by faith I had peace with God through our Lord Jesus Christ.[65] [¶]

After I had received the witness of my acceptance with God, I saw clearly that it was the free gift of God through faith. I saw a full and free salvation in Christ for the whole world, and I desired to tell what God had done for me, and what he was willing to do for all. I returned to the house filled with joy and peace to tell my wife what God had done for me, and that he was willing to pardon all her sins; and that if she would now give up her heart to him he would shed abroad his love in her soul.[66] She wept but seemed slow to believe. I left her to visit some mourners I had seen the day before. I went full of joy to let them know how they might be happy through faith in the Lord Jesus Christ. They also wept, but seemed slow of heart to believe and receive the blessing. I went on to the Baptist meeting. Mr. Morris, the minister I had conversed with the evening before, met me in the yard, gave me his hand, asking me how I felt today. I said, much better than I did yesterday. God has done great things for me this morning. He has set my soul at liberty and shed abroad his love in my heart[67] and I know now that I have peace with God. He said I saw in your countenance that there was a change of feeling.

I have been a little particular on this great and most interesting point – the witness of the conversion of the soul – being fearful that many rest short of it and rest on what is called a *hope*.[68] *Hope* is good – it is strengthening and cheering, when it looks forward to things to come; but it has no eyes behind – it cannot look backward to supply the place of a witness. There is a great difference between, I hope I *shall* be converted and I hope I am converted. I received a hope of the witness before I got it; but after I got it that hope was swallowed up in the enjoyment. I then hoped that I should endure to the end and be eternally saved; but had I rested and taken my hope for the witness, I should have remained in a most unhappy state. Let mourners say to their souls, Hope thou in God, for I shall yet praise him,[69] when he speaks peace to my soul; and believers cry, Come, and I will tell you what God has done for my soul; and then hope for holiness and heaven. And now, reader, I hope you will never rest if you have not got the witness in your heart that God, for Christ's sake, has pardoned your sins. Until you get it, take no man's word; no, not even the decision of a whole Church in your favor. Let nothing stop you, until Jesus speaks, "Go in peace, thy sins are forgiven thee."[70] Do not say, I hope I have religion; but press and pray on until God speaks to thy heart and thou canst say, I know that my Redeemer liveth.[71]

From *The New Orleans Christian Advocate*

MARCH 27, 1858

[1800b]

Having now obtained mercy of the Lord, I had a great desire for the salvation of my relations and neighbors, and whenever an opportunity offered I endeavored to admonish them to flee the wrath to come; and when I through fear or neglect, failed, I always felt guilty before God. I did not attempt to speak in public; but families or individuals I often tried to persuade to seek the Lord, and I thought I saw some good fruits, which encouraged me to go in that way. I now saw it my duty to join some branch of the Church of God, but knew not what to do. There was a Presbyterian, a Baptist, and a Methodist Church all near me; but to choose was the all absorbing point.[72] I was raised among the Baptists; my parents and many relations were Baptists; I liked the name and the mode of baptism best, and wished to please my relations, if I could please God in doing so. I was a little acquainted with the Methodists, and as far as I could judge I liked their liberal doctrines, their general spirit, and above all the life of religion I saw many of them had attained unto.[73]

I loved all the Lord's people, but so it was that I did love and fellowship those the most that I believed loved and worshiped God in the most spiritual manner; and I really thought the Methodist people in general the most zealous, loving followers of Christ. But I was in a strait what to do. I said, on my knees, "O Lord I am a child and thou art my father; do thou direct my steps in this thing and unite me to thy people where I may receive and do the most good." I went to hear all and to converse with all for several weeks; but still knew not the will of the Lord. The Baptists had a two days meeting, where the door was to be opened, members received, and baptised. I went prepared to join if the Lord opened any way, by filling my soul with his love and uniting my heart with that people. That day the preacher sang, prayed and preached, and I tried to pray and give my heart to God, to guide me according to his own will. The door was opened for experience. I drew near while two gave in and were received on old experiences. I sought the Lord for his love to be shed abroad in my heart as it had been in times past and I would join; but my poor heart grew harder and harder, so I stepped out of the house and felt better. I concluded to wait on the Lord, knowing and believing his choice would be best for me. We went to the water where baptism was administered and a door opened again for me; but I could not join, not having the spirit of union and love. I returned home in company with an aged Baptist member who chided me for quenching the Spirit in refusing to join. I told him all my heart meekly, and my reasons for not joining that day. We talked on doctrine, and he called me a Methodist.[74] I said if I was, God had made me one, for I knew very little about the people. Another asked me for my experience, and I gave it to him honestly. He said it was very good, as far as it went; but it was too short. You, said he, have only received forgiveness for all past and present sins.

Now, said he, when I received the pardon of my sins, God forgave all past, present and to come; all that I ever was to commit was forgiven.[75] I said there was a difference in our experiences: mine was "Go in peace and sin no more." I thought if Christ forgives all sins to come, the Pope is right and follows his Master, for he will give a passport to heaven to a man if he will come to his terms; and if Christ forgives all sins to come, the Pope is but a follower of Christ in doing as his Master does: *both are indulgent.*[76]

I endeavored, as I had received Christ Jesus, so to walk in him; but still had desires to unite with God's people in some Church. I went again to hear the Methodists. I felt well under preaching; class meeting came on and I arose to go out. One took me by the hand, saying, you are welcome to stay in the class room with us.[77] I said if it was no intrusion I should be glad to do so. He said sit down. I did so. While the examination was going on, the power of God was present to heal the wounds I had received from some who contend more about unprofitable doctrine than against sin.[78] My soul was fed that day among the people called Methodists, and my heart was truly united to them. The preacher then opened the door to receive members, making a few observations on the rules in the Discipline.[79] I felt the Spirit of the Lord uniting my heart to the people of that class, and I arose to my feet and said, I would be thankful if they would receive me into the Church, as God had united my heart with theirs. That beloved man, Samuel Parker, was present and we rejoiced together in heavenly places in Christ Jesus. Afterward he became an eminent and useful preacher; but has long since gone to his reward. I was received on trial[80] I think about two months after my conversion, and have reason to bless God that I ever found a place in the Methodist Church. O that I had been a member of that Church twenty years sooner. But thanks be to God that I am what I am and where I am. Glory to God, for his unspeakable goodness to me. I know and remember the time when I began to love him; but I hope I never shall end loving and praising his great and excellent name. O my soul, praise him!

When I returned home I told my wife that I had joined the Methodist Church that day. She said she was sorry that she had not been there, so that she might have joined with me; but she would shortly have an opportunity to join, when she did a few weeks after. She joined as a seeker, which was a great comfort to me.[81] I was happy among a people who lived in love, and met every Sabbath, either to hear preaching or pray, and speak to each other about the welfare of their souls. [¶]

I was somewhat troubled in mind about baptism by immersion – by my mind being biased in my raising in favor of that mode – after conversion.[82] I sought light on the subject by carefully reading God's word, with prayer. I found in doing so that John the Baptist was Christ's forerunner, and water baptism was administered by him before the Holy Spirit was given. Christ did not go before John to prepare the way before him by converting the soul and baptising with the Holy Ghost, but John went before Christ and baptised with water. Christ came after John and baptised with the Holy Ghost and with fire. I was surprised that I had been so much in the dark in reading the 3d. of Matthew, for I had viewed John following Christ, with the water to finish the work; but if we patronize John we must go as forerunners of Christ, preach and baptise with water and let Christ follow and finish the work, baptising with the Spirit.[83] [¶]

These things produced a change in my mind; and why, thought I, reject infants when Christ received them and declared them to be subjects of his kingdom.[84] In this he was a prophet, like Moses, who was commanded of God to bring them into the Church at eight days old. God is the same, his Church is the same, and we are only branches grafted into the original root that is holy. The root bears us and not we the root. Infants were natural branches of old, and must be yet, for Christ saith, "Of such is the kingdom of God, and let them come and forbid them not."[85] John the Baptist, our Lord's forerunner, and Christ himself were members of the visible Church at eight days old. These are examples to us that we may follow the same; but Christ being baptised at thirty years of age, was not to make him a member of the visible Church on earth, but to fulfill the righteousness of the law of which, in the sight of men, he was ordained to be a high priest and took on him an endless priesthood after the order of Melchisidec,[88] to make an atonement for us by the shedding of his own blood; and as he is the propitiation for the sins of the whole world,[87] all men, women and children ought to be and were appointed to be baptised in water, as a seal of the promise to them and to their children. And as Jesus Christ is that prophet, like unto Moses, all the world should submit to be baptised unto him as the Israelites were unto Moses. [¶]

After thinking seriously on these things and duly considering the nature of water baptism, I became perfectly satisfied that baptism was the setting the subject apart for God, and the sooner the better; and if done by a regular ordained minister of the Church of Christ and in the gospel form it was valid. I felt my conscience perfectly at ease on that subject ever after; and on reading God's holy word I saw that it was my duty to leave these things behind and to go on unto perfection, not laying again the foundation from dead works.[88]

From *The New Orleans Christian Advocate*

APRIL 3, 1858

[circa 1801]

I had a great desire for the salvation of my fellow men everywhere, and often spoke to them, as individuals or families, when an opportunity offered; persuading them to seek after the true religion of Christ, which was love. I had no thought of standing up before a congregation to preach, as I had no gifts. I believed God could make apostles and preachers out of fishermen or even plowmen, and that he could choose the foolish things of the world to confound the wise, and the weak things of the world to confound the mighty; that no flesh should glory in his presence, and that it might appear that the wisdom and power of the gospel of Christ was of God. We now had four promising children, and offered them all up to God in baptism. Rev. John Sale baptized them in the name of the Father and the Son and the Holy Ghost, putting this great name in their foreheads according to God's word: "And his name shall be in their foreheads" – (Rev. 22:4) "sealed in their foreheads" – (Rev. 7:3.) Two of them now are with their Savior in a better world. Glory to God for the promise which is to us and to our children, of a right to his Church on earth and then in heaven.

Forbid them not, ye good, mistaken disciples, for of such is the kingdom of God.[89] [¶]

Hearing of the great work of God, in Cumberland, West Tennessee, and land being good, cheap and plenty, I visited that country in the same fall. I liked it well, found many happy Christians, good societies, and my soul was refreshed among them. I prepared and removed by land 200 miles, and settled in a large, living society of Methodists, 40 miles above Nashville.[90] We gave our letters to Brother Lambuth,[91] the preacher in charge of the Nashville circuit. We felt happy in being thus highly favored of God. Our meetings were regular and powerful – many embracing religion and uniting in love at preaching, prayer, class meeting and love feast. Here I had pleasure of seeing and also of hearing Bishop Whatcoat, and Bishop Asbury; also, Wm. McKendree, the Presiding Elder; also.[92] John Magee, an old and useful preacher; shortly after, John Page and Thomas Wilkinson, men of God, all uniting at camp meetings and circuit preaching. Wherever they went, the great power of God attended their ministry, in the conversion of souls and in building up believers; all which added much to our own comfort and advancement in the knowledge of our Lord and Savior Jesus Christ. Yet, strange to tell, many, even professors in the Church, lived like the foolish virgins, having no oil in their vessels.[93] They could tell a fine experience when in their first love;[94] but alas for them, they had a name to live, while dead. I saw the danger of losing my first love and of living in a lukewarm state.[95] I therefore felt determined, by the assistance of divine grace, to seek a clean heart[96] which I desired above all things; for I was often troubled and tempted, especially after being very happy, that I had deceived myself and was not what I felt. I was troubled with evil thoughts, which I hated; but thought they must proceed from the heart; therefore my heart was not right before God. This gave me much pain until I could again receive the witness that the Lord was mine. I had a great desire to obtain the abiding witness which St. John speaks of, that I might doubt no more.[97]

About this time, I heard William McKendree preach a sermon that relieved me very much. His text was, "Blessed is the man that endureth temptation, for when he is tried he shall receive the crown of life, which the Lord hath promised to them that love him."[98] He reasoned well on this text, showing that Christ himself was tempted, yet without sin, and so were his true followers. Christ *thought* of sin when tempted, but rejected it, and was sinless: so we, when tempted as he was, might remain unspotted by rejecting the temptation. He said the devil was a spirit, and could act upon our spirits contrary to our wills; as matter acted on matter, so spirit on spirit, both to lead to unlawful deeds; but no sin is committed without the consent of the will. So he that endured the temptation, as Christ did in the wilderness, opposing the enemy with the sword of the Spirit, did not sin. The temptation was of the devil; to resist was to endure and of grace, and a righteous act. He proved all by quotations from the word of God, making out clearly every point in hand, so that fools could not err. He was a workman indeed, saying a great deal in a few words; so that the mind never grew weary under his preaching. His sermons always appeared too short, although as long as many others. This sermon gave me much strength, afterwards, in time of temptation, knowing how to resist and endure; but yet I had a hungering and thirsting for the abiding witness, that I might doubt no more, and that the love of God might remain in my soul, every moment, to the destruction of all sin – a sanctification of my soul, body and spirit.

About one year after my conversion, I was in class meeting and was called upon by the leader to pray. While praying on our knees, I thought of a woman who was expected to die, and did die that day. I earnestly entreated God on her behalf, that he would sanctify her soul before it left the body. And I felt assured that God would save her from all sin, and take her soul to heaven, and at the same time

I had the witness that God, for Christ sake, had given me a clean heart and that I should doubt no more.[99] At the same moment, I felt such a blessing as I had never felt before. It was indeed unspeakably glorious. At the same time the whole room seemed to be filled with the glory of God, and it was an uncommon time of rejoicing.

I felt a desire to tell my brethren what God had done for me. He had given me the witness of a clean heart and that I should doubt no more of the soundness of my conversion. I did tell them that I should doubt no more of the soundness and reality of my conversion to God: but when I was about to tell them that God then had saved me from all sin, by his free Spirit, sanctifying my soul, a thought struck me that they would not believe me, and that it would appear like boasting; and if my life after should not accord with my profession, it would be a reproach to the good cause. I refrained and I believe, in some degree, lost the blessing which God gave me; but as far as I confessed, that is that I could not doubt the genuineness and truth of my conversion at first and the comforts and blessings of the Holy Spirit, that it was of God, and no deception, so it has been ever since, now forty-one years. I have not doubted of my conversion, nor the first visitations of his Spirit. I am assured it is of God. As I received and confessed before men, so he has preserved me from those afflicting doubts ever since; but as I did not confess him in my sanctification from all sin, I have not always have that abiding witness.[100] God is good and very merciful, and has not cast me off, but gives me peace with him through our Lord Jesus Christ.

After receiving the above unspeakable blessing, I was greatly strengthened to go on to do the will of the Lord as far as I thought he had called me to speak or labor for him among my fellow men. About a year after my removal to Cumberland, I was appointed class leader by Brother Page, the preacher in charge. I thought myself too young in the faith and not qualified for the place; but I submitted, believing I ought to obey the authorities in the Church of God. I had reasons to believe that God was with me in our class and prayer meetings,[101] where we had good times, and souls were converted as well as under preaching. We had two circuit preachers, appointed that year, and then it was too large and laborious. A third was employed by the Elder, and now we had preaching every two weeks by the circuit preachers, John Page, Thomas Wilkinson and Jesse Walker, employed by the Elder.[102] Times were good this year in the Nashville circuit, and in the circuits adjoining. The Cumberland Presbyterians were all alive in the work in many places, preaching and communing together.[103] All was love. [¶]

I began to be deeply convicted about preaching and was advised by some of my brethren and the preachers to take license;[104] but I felt fearful of running before called. As a class leader I had the privilege to exhort, which I did; but my mind let me out after the salvation of all men. I had no rest, thought I was not qualified to preach, and that perhaps it was a temptation of the wicked one; this gave me great distress of mind. I was inwardly urge to try, and then I should know if it was of the Lord or not. I waited for a door to be opened that I might try and know whether God had called me, so that my mind might be at peace; for I was troubled by day with thoughts on the subject and by night with dreams. I went to a night meeting; but the preacher did not come and there was no one to speak to the people. One came to me and said, "You must speak to the people." Now, thought I, the way is open and I have said in my heart if the Lord opens the way I will try to preach and if the Lord owns me I shall know and obey. I went forward sang and prayed and with trembling took a text – "Come, for all things are now ready."[105] I endeavored to introduce, explain and apply the text, feeling much better and more liberty than expected, and the Lord was pleased to send his Holy Spirit among the people, and I rejoiced, with many others who praised God aloud. [¶]

I went home happy in God my Savior. Shortly after, my way was opened on the Sabbath, where a large congregation met to hear the Rev. John Magee; he did not come. Some of my brother pressed me to preach, as there was no other chance for the people. I consented, believing that God had again opened my way. I spoke on the parable of the great Supper in the Gospel by St. Luke, 14th chap. 16th including the 24th verse. That day I felt great liberty and had reason to hope good was done.[108] After this I was licensed by the Quarterly Conference, and have continued ever since, trying to preach Jesus and him crucified,[107] wherever my lot has been cast.

From *The New Orleans Christian Advocate*

APRIL 10, 1858

[circa 1802]

Some months before I received license to preach, my wife was converted to God at a night meeting, where the society met to pray together. She went on to meeting with a brother and sister Anderson, at my request, and I remained at home to take care of the children. When she started, I said, be sure to get religion before you return. After they went on, I went to secret prayer, and while praying for my wife that her soul might be converted, I had strong faith that she would return home happy in God. It was clear moonlight, and I was engaged in a little work, which I could see to do by moonlight. While at work I felt assured in my mind that God would convert my wife that night. I think my confidence was about as strong as that she would live to come home. The meeting continued late; I waited in great confidence until I heard them coming. I went on the road to meet them and rejoice with my wife, which was even so. The moment she saw me, she broke out afresh, giving glory to God for what he had done for her soul. This was a happy time with us both. Now we were of one heart and mind in spiritual things as well as temporal.

Not long after, our eldest daughter Elizabeth was brought to the knowledge of God, being only nine years of age. This was at a night meeting at my own house; all were satisfied, saint and sinner, that God had brought a powerful change on the soul of the little girl. Her experience and language, while declaring what God had done for her, was convincing. She lived in the Church through life, married and died in great peace. Glory to God for all these blessings. I followed farming, worked diligently to supply my little family. My wife and children were all industrious, and all went on well. We had three meetings every week and sometimes four, one on the Sabbath and two or three at nights. There was a great excitement, many convictions and conversions, which was a means of bringing the people together to these meetings; for even the thoughtless would go to see new things and be caught in the gospel net. Some would come to laugh at others for their weakness, and they themselves be taken suddenly by the power of God, and thrown down, and lie almost lifeless for hours; then awake praying for mercy, and after a while arise praising God and exhorting all around them who had not turned to God, to turn and live; and perhaps, in a few minutes after their own conversion, join in prayer for mourners, surprising all who heard them, for they prayed like old, experienced people or preachers. God put a new language into their mouths, never spoken by them before. Every mouth of opposition was stopped. Children of seven or eight years old told of the wonderful works of God. The old told how a man can be born again when he is old.[108] All this I have seen. Young, proud gentlemen and fashionable ladies would fall in the dust, cry to God for mercy, come through, and speak aloud with a boldness and a language unknown to themselves before. [¶]

This great work began, I think, in 1800, to be very general, yet it had been experienced among the Methodist people from the time of their first preaching in Tennessee and Kentucky. It had never produced such a great reformation and general excitement until the year 1800.[109] In the fall of the same year I witnessed at the camp meetings and the other meetings, such things as I had never seen before; but I had read of like or similar work in Europe and in America. Men of sound thinking and morals always acknowledged that the people were greatly reformed and made better under these extraordinary visitations, and every good man prayed, "O Lord, as it does so much good, send us more and more of it until the whole earth is filled with the knowledge of thy truth." But some of the mole- eyed opposers spoke evil of these things, and finding tares among the wheat, were for pulling up the wheat, because an enemy had sown tares in it.[110] They were for clean work, cutting down young corn because there was some grass and weeds among it. Such men know little, reason badly, and do much harm. Very few of this class were made subjects of the work of grace in this revival. One of them is wiser than seven men who can render a reason. Perhaps some even of these may find mercy, as we are commanded to pray for all men.

A blooming, daring, full-faced young woman, Mrs_, came to one of our camp meetings, saying on the way, When I get there and they begin to shout and cry glory to God I will shout glory to the devil and see how they will like that. She came; the work began in the meeting house; she arose and stood on one of the seats to do what she had promised; but her mouth was stopped and she fell on the floor, lay some time like a dead person, after which she cried out, "I am damned, I am damned; hell is my portion: there is no mercy for me. I am gone, eternally gone, hell is my portion." Christians prayed for her; but she still affirmed there was no mercy. She remained in this state for about twenty- four hours, in despair affirming there was no mercy for her, until her case really appeared hopeless. At last she began to pray for mercy, and God in great mercy spoke peace to her soul.[111] This case had a salutary effect on many. I witnessed her conversion, saw her sometime after happy in

God, and I hope she will prove faithful to him who brought her from the jaws of hell.

I saw a young man at this place, who had been very wicked; he was struck with a power which jerked him with great force.[112] He commenced a kind of dance, looking and talking hopelessly, saying, I have often danced to please myself but now God makes me dance against my will. After some time he fell and was carried off by his friends. Many cases of the same kind occurred, no person being able to tell us why it was so, not even those who were exercised so strangely. All they could say was, they believed God had sent it on them for their good. Some were so opposed to the exercise that they would not go where it was, and some of them took it at home. The professors and non-professors had it frequently.[113] It was not in consequence of new doctrine or excitement in the preaching of the gospel. I saw no difference in the present and former manner or doctrines, in the preachers or preaching; and all I can say about it is, I never felt it myself, but I believe God sent it on some for good. I felt resigned and said, the will of the Lord be done.

There were some things among the people at times which appeared miraculous. Once we met at the house of brother Baker, who was confined to his bed by the epidemic or influenza; his case appeared to be dangerous. A prayer meeting was agreed upon, and while prayer was made for him that God would heal and raise him up again, he arose from his bed, praised God, saying the Lord had healed him, and he was perfectly well. We continued sometime with him that night and left him as he said well and said afterward that he felt that affliction no more.

Another case: An old man, sixty years of age, was taken with the fever. Medicine failed; he and his family despaired of his recovering and sent for me to come pray for him. I did so in the morning. He asked me to preach there that night, and the appointment was circulated and the house filled at early candlelight. I read, sung and prayed; then read the text, "It is appointed unto men once to die, and after this the judgment."[114] I spoke of the certainty of death and judgment. I then pointed out the preparation for both, and while offering the atonement made by the blood and all-sufficient sacrifice of Christ, he began to praise God aloud in his bed. His friends and children gathered around him. I ceased to speak, as the house was filled with the praise of God. After a little time I went to the bedside; he reached out his hand to me saying, God has cured both my soul and body and I am now well and happy, and it was even so. His body was healed and his soul converted, all by believing in the Lord Jesus Christ. What was this? By what power was the man healed? All was done in an instant, the beholders being witnesses. The above is true, call it what you please. O God, I will praise thee – amen. This man's name was Williamson. [¶]

At another time I met a congregation of people, who had assembled for preaching and praying where a young woman was lying and expecting to die. Being somewhat of a stranger, the preacher, brother Copeland,[115] who lived in the settlement, pressed me to preach. I thought I would take the same text – "It is appointed unto man once to die," etc; and while preaching the Lord was powerfully present and the young woman proclaimed aloud that God for Christ's sake had forgiven all her sins and healed her afflicted body. And brother Copeland told me afterwards that she was raised up from that hour and made whole. Jesus Christ is the same yesterday, to-day, and for-ever.[116] All things are possible to him that believeth;[117] but without faith it is impossible to please God.[118] Many did not believe in these things, and spoke against those who do, calling them fanatics, etc.; and yet they visit the sick and pray for them that God may heal and raise them up again. What do they mean?

At another time a brother in Christ was brought to the door of death to all appearances; medical aid failed; he was deeply impressed that God would heal him if he would use the scriptural means pointed out by St. James.[119] Accordingly he proceeded to obey by sending for such as the word of God designated. When we came where he was he told us for what purpose he had sent for us. I said, if thou canst believe, all things are possible to him that believeth.[120] He said he did believe. We united in prayer for his recovery and he was strengthened in time of prayer to believe, and from that hour his pain and fever left him. He was very low and weak, but soon recovered health and strength, and professed to be made whole through faith in the Lord Jesus Christ, afterward testifying that Christ had yet power on earth to heal;[121] and why not if the promises have not failed? O, said a good brother to me, such things bring scandal on the Church when known in the world. What will the world say about us? I do not believe in miracles these days.[122] Said I, you preach in all your sermons, Only believe in the Lord Jesus Christ and thou shalt be saved; yea now, this moment, thou shalt receive the forgiveness of all thy sins and have peace with God. If we believe not in miracles, why preach them in public in the pulpit, and then deny them in the world? The cure of a bodily disease is great, but that of the soul much greater; if we receive not little things, how can we expect the greater. If running with the footmen weary us, how shall we contend with horsemen;[123] and if we receive not earthly things, how shall we believe the heavenly?[124] But according to thy faith be it unto thee.[125] We speak that we do know, and testify that we have seen.[126] The prayer of faith shall save the sick[127] and the Lord shall raise him up, and if he have committed sins they shall be forgiven him. These promises are yea and amen to him that believeth.

Again: it may be that God sees as man seeth not;[128] it may not be his will to heal or answer our prayers in that thing or case then; but after the man has suffered awhile. The prayer of faith may be answered sometime after; therefore we should be resigned and say, "Thy will be done." It is said by some it cannot be proved that any are cured or converted in answer to prayer, that might not have been without prayer. But this is saying too much; for God has said, The prayer of a righteous man availeth much,[129] and they that ask to them it shall be given,[130] and he that believeth not God has hath made *him* a *liar*.[131] It is a damning sin to say that God is not true and will not do what *he* has promised us. O beware of this great sin laying the blame on *Him* and excusing ourselves.[132] God cannot lie. Our faith may fail; but *his* promises cannot fail him that believeth. Then let us repent for our unbelief and say, "Lord increase our faith."[133]

From *The New Orleans Christian Advocate*

APRIL 17, 1858

[circa 1807]

After living about nine years in Tennessee, I removed to Missouri and settled in the township of Belview, near the lead mines.134 Here was work for more preachers than were in the country, traveling or local. I found two eminent men of God who were traveling preachers in that country – Samuel Parker and David Young. The former a Presiding Elder, the latter a circuit preacher, having the charge of the circuit in which I settled. This was in 1807. I was happy to meet the two brethren, as I had been acquainted with them in former years. The work of God had begun and was going on in that country before I removed there; but I had visited that part and preached to them the year before. Some of the preachers had been visiting them, a few times before; but little had been done. I was then a local preacher and had traveled one year on the Roaring river circuit in Tennessee, employed by the Presiding Elder, Rev. Wm. McKendree. I was an assistant preacher with brother Edge in care of the circuit. [¶]

Being in a strange country, I determined to unite my little labors with the good brothers above named, and before the year was ended there was a good work in that part of the circuit, though we had to contend with opposition of various kinds. God owned his word and many were, I trust, soundly converted, under the preaching of a free and full salvation[135] through faith in our Lord Jesus Christ, who tasted death for every man. Living societies were raised in the country, and one in the settlement of Belview where I lived, which was large and happy in love to God and each other, having the mind of Christ and fellowship with one another. Our camp meetings were fruitful; circuit preaching, prayer and class meetings were regular, and generally very lively, and the Church prospered. A few of our sheep were stolen, put under the water, went in and came out, no better in faith or practice; but lost their Christian fellowship and union with those they once loved. I believe they lost much and gained nothing, except that they now were not like other men, nor even as those Methodists. O what a change cold water makes on some men's feelings! But love is the fulfilling of the law.[136] The love of God and man is the bond of Christian union; and by this shall all men know that ye are my disciples if ye have love one to another. By their fruits ye shall know them.[137] What fruits? Love, joy, peace, long suffering, gentleness, meekness, temperance.[138] Not water, not immersion, which often separates those which God had joined together in love. May God save his flock from *him* who cometh not but for to *steal* and to *kill* and to *destroy*.[139] O when will Christians all rally around the standard of love and cease to judge and condemn one another on those non-essential points on which God has given every man liberty to think for himself.[140] Love will unite all against sin and for holiness. The Christian loves holiness, because it is of God. He hates sin, because it is of the devil. He that pleads for holiness pleads the cause of God. He that pleads for sin must be [the] devil's advocate. All doctrines, rules, practices, or usages in the church that tear asunder or keep apart those that love God and keep his commandments, are not of God.

True Christians all love one another, their peculiarities, by-rules, or a difference in opinions on points or doctrine not essential to salvation, notwithstanding. Nothing but a willful sin can exclude a brother from their communion.[141] The laws of God are, Ye shall or ye shall not – thou shalt in any wise or thou shalt in no wise. Thus we see when we refuse to obey a plain command we sin; but there is no plain command at what time we shall take the Lord's supper, whether by night or day, whether leaning, sitting, standing or kneeling, how much bread or wine we may take; but all is left optionary with the communicants; so also it is with baptism. We have no plain command, whether we shall use much water or little. Whether it shall be performed by night or day, in the house or in the wilderness, or how deep we must go in, or whether we must or must not go under, be poured upon, or sprinkled with clean water. As in the Lord's supper, so in baptism; as it is not the putting away the filth of the flesh,[142] it is therefore left to the conscience of them that receive it, as each receives for himself.

Reader, have I wearied you by saying so much about love. You will bear with me when I tell you that it is eternal life to my soul. It is the soul of my soul, and the life of my life. Give me that and I am eternally happy. I can ask nor want no more, and no less will do me. God is love, and he that dwelleth in love dwelleth in God and God in him.[143] O yes 'tis heaven to know my Savior.[144]

[1809]

The above doctrines, principles, and feelings of my heart, have been the reason I now give for trying to preach the gospel of Christ my Redeemer. His yoke has been easy and his burden light to me.145 When traveling through rains, snows, high waters, swamps and canebreaks, I have found the promise true – "Lo I am with you to the end of the world."146 I lived six years in the settlement of Belview,147 now Washington county, Mo., in which time I saw a great and good work, from the fall of 1809 until I left that country. The work of God gradually increased and grew up more and more, under the faithful labors of the Lord's servants who traveled among us. They were men called of God. Of this I have no doubt, as their fruits were abundant and testified that they were called of God to preach. Many of their names are yet dear to me; but none more so than that holy man, Samuel Parker, who presided there several years. He was an able minister of the truth, as it is in Jesus. On every point he was plain, pointed, clear and powerful; his arguments were almost irresistible; all that heard him seemed deeply interested, finding nothing to say against the man, his address or doctrines. Even when he reproved, he had the approbation of all; he used the sharp two-edged sword,148 but it was so tempered with kindness that every mouth was stopped. It is true, some said he was not much of a disciplinarian; but if I ever saw a man follow his blessed Lord and Master nearer in that one thing than brother Parker did, I do not know it. When I last parted with him I felt more than my tongue or pen can express, believing I should see him no more on earth; but my spirit was sustained by strong faith that we should shortly meet again and mingle our voices above as we had frequently done on earth. As brother Parker is now beyond the reach of flattery, there is no danger in speaking a little of his great worth. [¶]

Brother J. Walker was appointed Presiding Elder after brother Parker, and the good work of the Lord prospered under his care and labor, he was a useful man, a self-denying, cross-bearing, persevering soldier of the kingdom, leaving wife and children, houses and lands for the Lord's cause, yet providing for his household. He pressed on me the duty of receiving deacon's orders, as I had been elected to that office some years before in Tennessee, but had felt diffident and backward to take upon me that responsibility; for I really thought a license to preach the gospel as high a stand as I was qualified to fill; but at his request I submitted with trembling and was ordained, Bishop Asbury and Bishop McKendree officiating. This was a solemn day to me. Lord, pardon thy unworthy servant wherein he has come short of filling the place and office assigned him on that day. After this I felt bound to take heed to my ways as a servant of the Church of God, to do all and every thing required in the word of God and our good discipline for the advancement of the Church which Christ the Lord had purchased with his own blood. And so it was, the Lord was my helper in providing plentifully for my wife and ten children, and at the same time enabling me to spend a large portion of my time in traveling with the elders and preachers to the camp meetings, quarterly meetings, and through the country, getting and trying to do good.[149]

[1811-1812]

The great earthquake came on about the middle of December, 1811, about midnight, when the people generally were heavy with sleep.150 They were suddenly awaked, as if with the trump of God; for the earth reeled to and fro like a drunken man. Our houses seemed to jump and skip; the cattle and other beasts ran and roared; the fowls on the roosts screamed and fell to the ground; the trees trembled, as with fear, clasping each other in the arms of their long branches as if trying to lean on each other for help. Women and children, arising from sleep, fled to affrighted husbands and fathers for safety, while an awful sound of a subterraneous thunder rumbled beneath the ground, seeming to warn the unbelievers that hell was moving from beneath to meet them at their coming. They cried aloud to God to have mercy on them, beseeching the Christians, whose hearts and confidence was stayed on God, to pray for them. Some ran, like the trembling jailer,151 falling on their knees crying out aloud, "Oh father, pray for me." This was an awful night. Some leaving their own houses and running to their neighbors, pale, with death-looks in their countenances, inquiring,

"What is this that is coming upon us?" They saw no way of escape. The next morning was awful. One shock following another; the solid ground running in waves, resembling those on the face of the lake, in time of high winds. It really appeared as if the ground must be split and torn asunder by the dreadful convulsions that passed one after another; but God was with us, and I felt assured that we had a building eternal in the heavens that could not be shaken.152 That part of the country suffered but little when compared to that about New Madrid, where those shocks tore the earth asunder, changing the face of the country, raising lakes to dry land and timbered lands becoming wet and swamp lands, level beautiful prairies thrown into mounds and deep chasms. About this time it was easy to preach to the people; all seemed to be humbled and came together in crowds to hear what they must do to be saved. Many, I believe, were soundly converted while the earthquake influence lasted, which was, I think, for about three months, though not so severe as at first; only at times the shocks were felt. Afterward, when the danger seemed to be past, some forgot their promises and turned to their sins again.153

After bro. Walker, bro. Samuel W. Thompson was appointed as Presiding Elder and the good work of the Lord still prospered. What I mean by the good work of the Lord, was not merely taking in members, or as man changing his mind on notions about religion; but it was a spiritual change, wrought upon the hearts and souls of the people; so that they obtained the witness of sins forgiven through faith in our Lord Jesus Christ and the love of God shed abroad in their hearts by the Holy Spirit sent down from heaven. This witness was generally preceded by a deep conviction of sin and a cry for mercy to Him that was able to save. And frequently many would crowd to the altar, where prayer was made for them, and they would arise filled with love, joy, and peace giving glory to God for his mercy to them.

From *The New Orleans Christian Advocate*

APRIL 24, 1858

[1813 or 1814][154]

In the fall of the year 1813 while I was living in the township of Bellview, Mo.,[155] following farming, by which I was enabled to support my family decently and to labor as a local preacher, my brother, James Stevenson, who then lived on the Ouachita river, now state of Arkansas, Clark county, visited me and remained a few weeks with us; and seeing the great advantage of a preached gospel among the people, he lamented the condition of the wilderness settlements of the Ouachita, Red river, and Forte Caddo, where he lived, and also the settlements of White river and many other settlements on the smaller streams of the West. These bounds were about four hundred miles in length and at least, on an average, one hundred in breadth. While conversing with him I saw, as he described it, a vast region sitting in darkness and the shadow of death, scattered like sheep on the mountains, having no shepherd to guide their feet into the way; none to say, Behold the Lamb of God, that taketh away the sin of the world.[156] I felt a great desire for the salvation of those destitute people, and was pressed by my brother to go home with him, see the people, and preach to them.

He hoped also that I might like the country and move to it. I agreed to accompany him. [¶]

We prepared for the journey, it being about four hundred miles, mostly wilderness except on the rivers and rich lands, where we found settlements of industrious people; but among them many hunters, for wild game, buffalo, bear, deer, beaver, etc., were common. All were alive to their calling and we found them friendly and humane. Prayer in families and the gospel preached was a new thing; but all, with few exceptions, received us, joined in family prayer, or at least had nothing against it, and truly my soul was happy in praying with and speaking to them on the importance of providing for the soul as well as the body. Our journey was a pleasant one. Sometimes we camped in the wilderness, by a running stream, the water and range for our horses good; and sometimes we found room in the friendly man's cabin, shared with him in the fruits of his chase, belled our horses, turned them out in a large pasture of the wilderness, had prayers with the family, laid ourselves down on a bear or deer skin, slept soundly and arose happy. At some places we found good beds and better fare; but all was well, for God was with us. [¶]

At length we arrived in the settlement where my brother lived, but did not reach his home before night, but stayed at the house of Mr. F. McMahon, who had once been a member of the Baptist Church in Kentucky. He had greatly backslidden. At the moment I was introduced to him by my brother, he looked wild and somewhat surprised, and said within himself, Is it possible that God has sent a preacher among us? This I learned of him afterwards. He was kind, fed us and our horses, and his wife also received us cheerfully. All soon became acquainted, conversation free and social; but turning on the subject of religion, he appeared not rightly to understand the gift that had come upon all men unto justification of life. After hearing the word of God read on those points, I saw joy spring up in his eyes; for he had been for several years nearly in despair, and truly it is good news to hear that Christ died for all. Night came on, we proposed to have prayer; all was right and when we kneeled to pray, I felt like God was near, for Mr. McMahon cried aloud for mercy; his wife wept, and some of his children, the oldest in particular. Here the work began in this family; they were evidently the first fruits of my labors in that part now called the state of Arkansas.

Next Sunday I had an appointment at Mr. Cumming's, a few miles below on the Forte Caddo, a branch of the Ouachita. The congregation was respectable, and before meeting commenced I was introduced to an old mother in Israel, a widow indeed, late from the States. Her name was M. Dickson. She appeared delighted to hear that God was mindful of the country in sending the gospel to them. While preaching that day to a desirous looking people, the good spirit was among them; some were deeply affected, and cried for mercy. The old widowed mother rejoiced in God her Savior, and there appeared to be a good work beginning, and so it was, for the fruits are yet seen even in 1841.[157]

Thus the Lord opened the way. We know that without Him men labor in vain; but all the promises are yea and amen to them who believe on, trust in and obey Him. From this settlement I went westward, visited the settlements and preached on the Turnwaw,[158] Wolf Creek, Little Missouri, and Mound Prairie, and was greatly comforted in having reason, from what I saw and heard, to believe that God had called his servants the preachers to spread the gospel through this vast territory now settled and settling fast. The people had made a great many small settlements all through the country from five to twenty miles apart. No wagon roads yet laid out, as they had generally moved on pack horses; nothing but horse-paths, many of them along the buffalo road or trails, rivers, large creeks, etc. No ferry boats, except on one or two rivers. We had to cross by canoes or rafts, or on horse back. Hence, I saw a great difficulty in getting men who would be willing to face all these difficulties to carry the gospel to this people; and when they pressed me hard to come, or get some of the preachers from the Illinois Conference[159] to come and preach to them, I said, being a preacher, I could not tell what the Conference would do for them, but if I could not get a preacher sent to them, I would return next fall and stay as long as possible with them.

While I remained among them I visited families, preached when and where I could; but after having labored six or eight weeks with them I left them, having made up a few little societies. I left them, commending them to God and the word of his grace. I left them with a heart truly mixed with joy and sorrow. I rejoiced that God had begun a good work among the people in the wilderness; but to part with them and leave no help, none to look over them was heart- rending. I was not without comfort even in this case, for I did believe that the great Shepherd of Israel would take care of those lambs. A goodly number of mourners were inquiring what they must do to be saved. I had to leave them; but not without hope for their welfare. And so it was. Glory to God, I found many of them, after one year's absence, in the highway.

Returning to my family in the dead of winter, I found I had taken a violent cold, which was followed by acute rheumatism, which lasted nine or ten weeks, a great part of which time my pains were past description. I was happy in knowing that they were not eternal. Then even could I sing,

O what are all my sufferings here,
If Lord thou count me meet,
With that enraptured host to appear,
And worship at thy feet.[160]
God raised me up and I was again able to labor
on my farm and attend camp meetings
and other meetings as formerly.

[1814 or 1815]

At home with my family in the spring of 1814,[161] I had not forgotten my promise to the people of the Red river, Ouachita and Arkansas, White Spring and Current rivers, with many of less note. Having a sufficiency of the things of this world to sustain us comfortably, I felt it my duty to travel and preach in the country where I then lived, and bro. Samuel Thompson being Presiding Elder, a man whom I loved, invited me to travel with him, as I had done with bro. Parker and bro. Walker, to quarterly and camp meetings. I accepted bro. Thompson's offer and accompanied him to his camp and other meetings, which were always a blessing to me. This summer, while in company with bro. Thompson, I frequently spoke to him about Arkansas country, where I had been the fall before, hoping he would speak to the Conference and particularly the Bishop to send a preacher to those growing and promising settlements, telling of the extent of fine country, good land, excellent water and navigable streams, all of which discharged their waters into the Mississippi river, and which must shortly become a fine state, and I thought the gospel should begin with its youth. He consented to the propriety of sending them a preacher; but thought it was hardly possible, as the Conference was young and weak in members and the work already taken in by them was so extensive; but he advised me to join the Conference and travel some of these circuits already formed, as they could not all be filled. I said I had got my consent to do so, but could not, for I had promised the people in those wilds of Arkansas and Red river to visit them again, and if I had joined the Conference I should not be sent there and they would be left out. He then proposed that if I did go to that country in a few weeks, as I said I must, to keep my promise, he would, with my consent, have my name enrolled on the minutes as a traveling preacher. So it was, I joined Conference as a traveling preacher, while in the wilderness of the Arkansas, five hundred miles from the Conference when it was done.[162] I traveled six months in Arkansas, returned to the Bellview Circuit,[163] got home on Friday and my appointments were made before I arrived to begin on the next Sunday at the meeting house where I lived. I rested one day and started again, the next being the Sabbath and rode the Bellview circuit the balance of the year.

[1814-1815, or 1815-1816]

I proceed to give some account of the work in Arkansas. I left my family early in the fall of 1814, in company with bro. Joseph Reed, a local preacher and Bro. John Johnson, a professor of religion and husband of my eldest daughter. We had a pleasant journey to the new circuit which I intended to form and travel, beginning on the South side of the Current, about one hundred miles from my family, and extending southwest 400 miles to Pecan Point on the southwest side of Red River – a settlement of Americans in the bounds of the province of Texas.[164] Here I formed a Methodist society in the same year; but on our journey we commenced where we could get a few people to preach to, exhort and pray with. Bros. Reed and Johnson were great helpers while they remained with me; but they were looking at the country and stayed but a few weeks with me. We found wherever we preached the Lord was there and the people received us gladly. [¶]

It would be too tedious to speak of one-tenth of the various things, the privations and joyful meetings, conversions, etc., of this six months tour among this people. The work of the Lord had begun on the waters of Ouachita last year; but this year it extended from the Ouachita east to the Current river and west to the Pecan Point on the Texas side. We got up small societies on the rivers and large creeks where the people had found good land, stock range, etc. Most of the rivers were at the time without ferry boats; of course we were compelled to swim our horses by the side of canoes or rafts, with our saddle bags on our shoulders. I had not appointments so many as we had in years following; yet whenever there was hearers I attended as far as in my power, and almost in every place the word found access, for the Lord was present and had given the hearing ear and the understanding heart. The gospel was glad tidings to those people, who were generally honest, humane, industrious and peaceable, and but very few of them had yet learned to be quibblers about foreknowledge, unconditional election and final perseverance. In death, many of them received the end and fruits of their obedient faith – the salvation of their souls. They left us and have gone to rest, testifying that Jesus was with them in the valley and shadow of death. These were the first fruits of the gospel in many places throughout the then wilderness country, but now the state of Arkansas. [¶]

I must say in truth, to the credit of the first settlers of Arkansas, that they as a people in general, would have been no discredit to the better part of the community of the most respectable of the old or new world. And even those who did not unite with us in the Church had sound reason and good sense and courage to know and say that the gospel of Christ was the only means which God generally made use of to civilize, moralize, and christianize a country; therefore, they received us and freely gave us such things as they had. I have never seen harder times than these people had to encounter, while I was traveling and preaching to them. That year provisions were scarce indeed. The drought had ruined their crops; there was not bread for the people in the country; no market near to supply them; no boats then running. But being a firm, resolute, soldierly people, they endured all with patience. Some of them went far up the rivers into the prairies and returned with meat; others, destitute of horses to travel on, hunted about home, lived on deer, fish, and such things as they could find; but all these afflictions never prevented them attending the meetings. They came from afar, heard and received the word with joy, and so it was that the preacher and the people suffered and rejoiced together. [¶]

April 24, 1858

[1816]

At one of my appointments on Wolf Creek, I was hindered from going on my way for several days; but having formed a society there some time before, with some conversions and a goodly number of mourners, we had meeting every day; for I had brother McMahon with me as an exhorter, whom I had licensed, and he was warm in love. Here we labored day and night while we stayed and the word was fruitful. One poor Indian, a Choctaw, was converted under preaching; he could speak but little English, but I saw by his looks that he understood truth, at least to make him tremble and weep; and while some of the people were crying for mercy and others praising God for what he had done for them, the Indian received the Spirit of joy and peace in the forgiveness of sins. He came to me, took hold of my hand, looked up and by signs told me that the Great Spirit had come down into his heart and he now loved him. This he told in his own tongue to an interpreter. Afterwards he was always glad to see me. I saw him a year after, with some eight or ten Choctaws; he ran to meet me, held me by the hand, spoke to the others, and they all came up and took me by the hand and, in their tongue, called me brother. None can tell how I felt on this interview. Bro. McMahon frequently accompanied me to the different appointments where we had two or three days meetings. My design is only to give an outline of what I know of the planting of Methodism in the state of Arkansas. This year I found one local preacher on Spring river, bro. Henry Stevenson.[165] He was preaching in that settlement with acceptance, and removed, I think in the fall of 1816, to Ozan or Mount Prairie[166] settlement and was useful in the good work afterwards. Thus the work of the Lord took its start in that new country.

[1841]

Still I am trying to labor in the good work of the Lord, which has been life to my soul for forty years. I am now in the 73d year of my age,167 and waiting, in great confidence, for the fulfillment of the promise of that crown which the Lord hath laid up for all them that love his appearing. Amen. W.S.

NOTE BY ANOTHER[168]

We spend our years as a tale that is told – here ends this one. It had its trials, its blessings, its dark and its bright days – changes of season, society, time and place – all necessary for such probation as ours. Like a silver thread, grace runs through all this experience. Grace makes its charms and worth. Grace had its triumphs and finally ended in glory.

The experience of such lives, simply and truthfully put forth, form the basis of the safest and largest inductions, as to the nature of experimental religion.

On the 5th of March, 1857, at the house of his son-in-law, Major Dyer, in Claiborne parish, La., the good old man died, in the 89th year of his age. Long had he been waiting, in patience, for the change. After being speechless three or four days, he raised his shriveled and wrinkled arms in bed, smote them together and said, "Heaven's just up yonder! Come, Lord Jesus, come quickly" – then died.

NOTES

1. Walter N. Vernon pointed out a discrepancy in Stevenson's account of his preaching in Texas. Stevenson said that the preaching tour that included Texas was in 1814 and that while he was on this tour, his name was entered in the rolls of the Tennessee Annual Conference as an itinerant preacher. But the printed conference Journal shows that Stevenson was received as an itinerant in the fall of 1815, leading Vernon to suppose, on very good grounds, that the preaching in Texas was actually in 1815 rather than 1814: Walter N. Vernon, "Beginnings of Methodism in Arkansas," *The Arkansas Historical Quarterly* 31:4 (Winter 1972), 358, n. 6. See also the notes on the heading "1813 [or 1814]" below.
2. Walter N. Vernon, *William Stevenson: Riding Preacher* (Dallas: SMU Press, 1964), 38-40, 65-66.
3. A portion of the *Autobiography* relating to Arkansas (including the account of preaching in Texas) was published with Vernon's notes in his article on "Beginnings of Methodism in Arkansas," 358-365.
4. On these typical stages in the "way of salvation," cf. Ted A. Campbell, *Wesleyan Beliefs: Formal and Popular Expressions of the Core Beliefs of Wesleyan Communities* (Nashville: Kingswood Books, 2010), 147-166, and on the precedents for these stages of Christian experience in Puritan thought and in the thought of John and Charles Wesley, 67-70, 73-82, 107-115.
5. On the importance of the means of grace in Wesleyan and Methodist cultures, cf. Campbell, *Wesleyan Beliefs*, 30-32, 34-35, 171-172.
6. This seems confused. There is a city of Bastrop, Louisiana, in Morehouse Parish, but not a parish by that name. According to other accounts, Stevenson died in Claiborne Parish, Louisiana. See the note at the end of the *Autobiography*.
7. Ninety-Six is a town in Greenwood County, South Carolina, founded in the eighteenth century and so named because it was believed to have been ninety-six miles from the first Cherokee settlement to the west.
8. Stevenson reflects here the dialectic in east-coast Protestant churches following the First Great Awakening. Advocates of the Awakening supported enthusiastic religious expressions, traditionalists viewed them with great suspicion.

9. Psalm 145:9.
10. II Peter 3:9.
11. Stevenson enunciates here a consistent thread of Methodist teaching in opposition to Calvinism. Methodists understood the doctrine of predestination to contradict the goodness of God by attributing to God the intention to condemn human beings; cf. Campbell, *Wesleyan Beliefs*, 112-113, 141, 221-223. John Wesley made a similar argument in his sermon on "Free Grace," ¶ 23; in Albert C. Outler, ed., *Sermons* (Bicentennial Edition of the Works of John Wesley; four volumes; Nashville: Abingdon Press, 1984- 1987), 3:554.
12. I.e., women; I Peter 3:7.
13. Consistent with folk expressions of Methodist teachings, Stevenson uses the expression "I had not religion" to mean that he had not been converted and thus did not have the direct assurance of God's Spirit that his sins were forgiven, "the witness in themselves." Cf. Charles Wesley's hymn beginning "Spirit of faith, come down," which has the lines, "Inspire the living faith / (Which whosoe'er receives, / The witness in himself he hath, / And consciously believes)"; in the *Collection of Hymns for the Use of the People Called Methodists* (1780), hymn 83; in Franz Hildebrand and Oliver Beckerlegge, eds., *A Collection of Hymns for the Use of the People Called Methodists* (Bicentennial Edition of the Works of John Wesley, volume 7; Nashville: Abingdon Press, 1983), 183.
14. Matthew 8:25.
15. Romans 8:15. "Bondage," i.e., bondage to sin, was another characteristic term utilized by Methodists to describe the state of the soul prior to conversion; cf. John Wesley's sermon on "The Spirit of Bondage, and of Adoption," introduction, ¶ 2; in Outler, ed., *Sermons*, 1:250.
16. This should probably read "eighteen years of age." He says at the beginning of the *Autobiography* that he was about 20 years of age when he first heard a Methodist preacher. In the paragraphs following immediately after this one, he states that he heard a Methodist preacher about two years after the event described here. I am indebted to a student, Tammy Heinrich, who pointed out this inconsistency.
17. Another characteristic of folk Methodism, inherited from John Wesley himself, was the belief that almost every event in life was the deliberate result of divine intervention.
18. In this case, a "sleeper" denotes a ground-level support for a floor joist.
19. Matthew 17:10; Luke 17:6.

20. Zechariah 3:2. The term "a brand plucked from the burning" carried considerable weight in Methodist lore as a term that John Wesley had used of himself, for example, in his personal seals.
21. Methodist literature from this period consistently speaks positively of "solemnity" or seriousness. This was understood to be an appropriate religious affection along with penitence, joy, resolution, etc.
22. John 15:6.
23. Matthew 7:13.
24. James Fowler was literally Stevenson's uncle, as he indicates at the beginning of the next section below.
25. Rev. Fowler here describes Methodist belief in the "amissibility of grace," that is, the possibility of losing faith and forfeiting justification after conversion. Folk Methodism sometimes also referred to this as "falling from grace" (cf. Galatians 5:4); cf. Campbell, *Wesleyan Beliefs,* 152, 156. This belief stood in contrast to Baptist (and Presbyterian) belief in the "eternal security of the believer," popularly described as "once-saved, always- saved."
26. Stevenson's statement, "let creeds be reasonable" echoes the sentiments of John Wesley and other Methodist leaders. He also echoes the common sentiment in folk Methodism that a test of true religion is its practical effects, that is, whether it is able to lead people to faith and holiness.
27. Walter N. Vernon identifies the preacher as either Reuben Ellis, who had served as a presiding elder in South Carolina after 1790, or his brother Ira Ellis; cf. Vernon, *William Stevenson*, 6.
28. Cf. Vernon, *William Stevenson*, 6.
29. Hebrews 2:3.
30. Mark 3:17; the expression "son of thunder" frequently appears in descriptions of dynamic, emotional Methodist preachers.
31. Early Methodist literature often refers to sinners, i.e., those who have not yet experienced conversion, as "crying out for mercy" as an indication that divine grace was working in them.
32. Romans 7:24.
33. Here Stevenson indicates a consistent critique of Baptists, objecting to their insistence that one must profess a conversion experience before joining with a congregation. Stevenson will argue throughout the *Autobiography* that this is a "youth- destroying" practice because it keeps people out of the Christian community when they most need it, namely, when they are seeking a conversion experience.

34. That is to say, the Methodist system encouraged "seekers," those who had not yet professed conversion to be part of their societies, in contrast to Baptist congregations.
35. Stevenson uses the term "professors" to denote those who "profess religion," i.e., who testify to a conversion experience.
36. This is a very frank expression of the typical motivation for westward migration.
37. Stevenson indicates that even at this point his uncle feared that young Stevenson would be corrupted by Methodist teachings (Arminianism).
38. The Blue Ridge is the first (easternmost) range of the Appalachians. The Iron Mountains are a range of the Appalachians near the intersection of Virginia, Tennessee, and North Carolina.
39. John Wesley had died in March of the previous year in London.
40. The Watauga and Nolichucky Rivers in western North Carolina and Eastern Tennessee.
41. Then a part of western North Carolina, Tennessee became a state four years later in 1796.
42. "Singing schools" originated in colonial New England as Reformed churches began to adopt "regular style" singing, that is, singing in parts as contrasted with the "usual way" which involved only unison singing. Singing schools typically employed the fa-sol method of teaching musical notation, and they became a fundamental aspect of Southern US culture, later regularized in such manuals as *The Sacred Harp* (1844).
43. Hezekiah Balch (1741-1810, not to be confused with a cousin named Hezekiah James Balch) was a well-known Presbyterian clergyman from this era. He had attended Princeton College between 1758 and 1762, and he was one of the founders of Tusculum College. His view of predestination was influenced by that of Samuel Hopkins, hence Stevenson's later comment that "he was a predestinarian; but moderate" (see later in the same paragraph). He was also known to be an opponent of slavery, as many people in eastern Tennessee were.
44. I Timothy 2:4.
45. Stevenson does not name his wife in this account. She was Jane Campbell from Augusta County, Virginia. In this period, Augusta County included a huge range of land in the Shenandoah Valley; cf. Vernon, *William Stevenson*, 12-13.
46. Romans 8:7.
47. Luke 11:21.
48. Cf. Romans 7:21 and ff.

49. Stevenson participated in the "means of grace" as he was seeking the conversion experience, consistent with Methodist teachings from the time of Wesley, who, in contention with the views of a group of eccentric London Moravians, had defended the use of the "means of grace" even for those who had not yet experienced the assurance of pardon; cf. Campbell, *Wesleyan Beliefs*, 30-32, 34, 171-172, 240.
50. Matthew 7:7, Luke 11:9.
51. Matthew 8:25.
52. Cf. Romans 8:14-17 where Paul described the grace of being a child and heir of God and contrasts "the spirit of bondage" with "the spirit of adoption."
53. Again, Stevenson's reflection seems guided by the insights of Romans 8, in this case Romans 8:16, "The Spirit itself beareth witness with our spirit, that we are the children of God."
54. In the older or British sense in which "want" means "lack" or "need."
55. Stevenson did not find satisfying Rev. Morris's claim that Morris had never had any deeper experience of assurance than Stevenson himself claimed. Later in this section Stevenson would exhort readers not to stop until they experience the full assurance of pardon.
56. The printed text in the *New Orleans Christian Advocate* has "grave" here, but Stevenson meant "grove," as he wrote a few words later in the same sentence.
57. Revelation 1:5.
58. Romans 8:16.
59. John 3:36.
60. I John 4:16.
61. II Corinthians 5:17. This is Stevenson's account of his own experience of conversion accompanied by his sense of the assurance of pardon.
62. I John 4:19.
63. II Corinthians 9:15.
64. Romans 3:26.
65. Romans 5:1.
66. Romans 5:5.
67. Romans 5:5.
68. Here Stevenson exhorts readers not to be content with a mere "hope" of justification, but to seek the full experience of assurance. Those familiar with John Wesley's theology will know that Wesley allowed "exceptional cases" in which persons were justified apart from the full assurance of pardon; cf. Campbell, *Wesleyan Beliefs,* 106-107, 113-114, 155, 159-161, 226-229. Stevenson does not seem to allow such "exceptional cases," and his work

is representative of a strain of folk Methodism that continued to claim that without the experience of assurance, one is not truly justified.

69. Psalm 42:11.
70. Luke 7:48.
71. Job 19:25.
72. Frontier religion in the US South in this period consisted largely of Presbyterian, Baptist, and Methodist groups. Presbyterians represented the inherited religion of Scots-Irish settlers in the southern and southwestern regions of the US, though frontier Presbyterianism was deeply revivalistic and contrasted with the staid Presbyterianism if the Atlantic coast. Only later would Disciples and Churches of Christ, then Holiness and Pentecostal groups, become prominent among southern US Christian communities.
73. Stevenson's reference to Methodists' "liberal doctrines" indicates that the term "liberal" was not at all a negative term in this period, and he indicates that even within folk-Methodist culture there was a spirit of liberality; cf. John Wesley's sermon on a "Catholic Spirit," in Outler, ed., *Sermons*, 2:81-95.
74. Stevenson's Baptist friend identifies Stevenson's own views as those of Methodists.
75. Stevenson's friend enunciates the Baptist (and Cumberland Presbyterian) belief in the "eternal security of the believer." Stevenson's objections to this belief will be a ground of his decision to become a Methodist.
76. Folk Protestantism had developed a belief that the Catholic practice of granting indulgences implied a guarantee of forgiveness for future sins. Stevenson thus attempts in a clever way to identify the Baptist teaching of eternal security with the Catholic practice of indulgences, but his argument relies on one of the most consistent of Protestant misunderstandings of Catholic practices of penance and indulgences.
77. Methodist class meetings were open to all who had "a desire to flee from the wrath to come, and to be saved from their sins" (as expressed in the General Rules). This implied that seekers (those who had not experienced conversion, and those who had not yet joined a Methodist group, were welcome to attend class meetings.
78. The "examination" refers to the central practice of the class meeting in which participants were examined regarding their fidelity to their promise to keep the General Rules. Stevenson found this exercise to be more fruitful than arguing about disputed points of doctrine.
79. That is, the General Rules (see the previous notes).

80. Methodist participants were received at first as "trial" or "probationary" members of classes, then upon the recommendation of the class leader they were enrolled as regular members of the class and admitted to the local society.
81. That is, she joined the class as one who had not yet experienced conversion and assurance. Stevenson is building his case that this practice of Methodist "liberality" toward seekers was one of the most important reasons why he found Methodist communities superior to Baptists and Presbyterian ones.
82. Stevenson clarifies that his concern here is not so much the issue of immersion itself, but the issue of whether he should be rebaptized following his conversion experience.
83. This is Stevenson's case for baptizing prior to conversion, and thus his case against the need for rebaptism following a conversion experience.
84. Now Stevenson turns to the issue of infant baptism, and argues consistent with what he says through the *Autobiography*, that it is better to form children in faith by baptizing them and thus including them in the Christian community than to wait until they have professed a conversion experience to baptize them.
85. Luke 18:6.
86. Hebrews 7:17.
87. I John 2:2.
88. Hebrews 6:1.
89. Matthew 19:14; Luke 18:16.
90. The area where he settled was then in Trousdale County (now Smith County), Tennessee, northeast of Nashville; cf. Vernon, *William Stevenson*, 17-18. This country was "above" Nashville in the sense that it was higher up the river.
91. Rev. William Lambuth, presiding elder in the Cumberland circuit; cf. Vernon, *William Stevenson*, 18-19, 24.
92. As a result of the itinerant system in use, Stevenson was in direct touch with the most influential leaders of the Methodist movement in North America. McKendree become the fourth bishop of the Methodist Episcopal Church (after Coke, Asbury, and Whatcoat) in 1808.
93. Matthew 25:1-13.
94. Revelation 2:4.
95. Revelation 3:15-16.
96. A typical Methodist expression denoting entire sanctification or Christian perfection.

97. The reference seems to be to John 14:16. Stevenson seems to equate entire sanctification with the "abiding witness" of the Spirit, that is to say (if I understand him correctly) with conversion one only has a temporary sense of pardon or assurance, but entire sanctification brings the "abiding" or permanent "witness." This does not seem to be a teaching derived from the Wesleys, though I sense that it became a standard feature of nineteenth-century folk-Methodist belief that was then taken up into the Holiness movement.
98. James 1:12.
99. This is Stevenson's testimony to his experience of entire sanctification, using the expression "a clean heart," which became one of a number of Methodist code words to denote the experience of entire sanctification or Christian perfection.
100. Consistent with the belief he expressed above, Stevenson claims that since the time of his experience of entire sanctification he had had a consistent sense of divine presence, though he believed that because of his early failure to testify to the experience of entire sanctification, he had not had the "abiding witness" of the Spirit consistently.
101. "Prayer meetings," typically segregated by gender, seem to have continued the "band meetings" that were part of the earlier Wesleyan movement in Britain.
102. Stevenson alludes to the fact that preaching by an itinerant or traveling preacher was relatively rare in early American Methodist groups.
103. Cumberland Presbyterian churches originated on the US frontier in this period, rejecting the doctrine of limited atonement, but maintaining (as Baptist groups would also maintain) the "eternal security" of those who have been converted.
104. License to preach.
105. Luke 14:17.
106. The expression "felt great liberty" was frequently used by Methodist preachers to describe their sense of inspiration while preaching.
107. I Corinthians 2:2.
108. John 3:4.
109. The revival of 1800 has been well documented in American religious history; cf. Vernon, *William Stevenson*, 20-24.
110. Matthew 13:24-30.
111. Psalm 85:8.
112. The experience described as "the jerks" has been common in American revivals since this time and was described in Peter Cartwright's

Autobiography describing this period: in W. P. Strickland, ed., *The Autobiography of Peter Cartwright: The Backwoods Preacher* (New York: Carlton and Porter, 1857) 48-51. Stevenson's attitude was that such experiences should be tolerated as long as they lead to holiness and fellowship.

113. Meaning those who had "professed religion," i.e., professed a conversion experience, as well as those who had not.
114. Hebrews 9:27.
115. It became common practice among Methodists (and perhaps other Protestant groups?) in the USA to refer to clergy as "Brother" followed by the surname.
116. Hebrews 13:8.
117. Mark 9:23.
118. Hebrews 11:6.
119. James 5:14; the elders of the church should anoint him with oil and pray for him.
120. Mark 9:23.
121. Cf. Mark 2:10.
122. Healing as a result of prayer, "faith healing," was a prominent part of folk Methodist culture and came to prominence in the subsequent Holiness and Pentecostal movements.
123. Jeremiah 12:5.
124. Cf. John 3:12.
125. Matthew 9:29.
126. John 3:11.
127. James 5:15.
128. I Samuel 16:7.
129. James 5:16.
130. Matthew 7:7.
131. I John 5:10.
132. In this case, as at the conclusion of many of the sections of his *Autobiography*, one can hear Stevenson's concluding oratorical pleas with his hearers or readers.
133. Luke 17:5.
134. The area he describes is now spelled "Bellevue," in Washington County, Missouri, where lead had been mined even prior to the area becoming part of the United States as a result of the Louisiana Purchase (1803).

135. The expression "free and full salvation" becomes a succinct summary of distinctive Methodist teachings: salvation is "free" in that it is available to all, and "full" insofar as it entails entire sanctification.
136. Romans 13:10.
137. Matthew 7:20.
138. Galatians 5:22.
139. John 10:10.
140. Stevenson's passionate plea to avoid disputes over "non-essential" doctrines gives another evidence of his sense of Methodist "liberality" and again echoes Wesley's sermon on a "Catholic Spirit," in Outler, ed., *Sermons*, 2:81-95.
141. Wesley had distinguished between "willful sin" and sins that could be the result of ignorance or weakness of the body or of the mind. He allowed that willful sins might remain in believers after justification: cf. Randy Maddox, *Responsible Grace: John Wesley's Practical Theology* (Nashville: Kingswood Books, 1994), 163-165. Although Wesley seemed to be unaware of it, the distinction is very similar to that drawn in traditional Catholic theology between "mortal" and "venial" sins, since "mortal sins" involve the full complicity of the will. Stevenson's point here is that only willful sins should be grounds for division between true Christians.
142. I Peter 3:21.
143. I John 4:16.
144. This expression scans like a line of poetry, but I have not discovered its source.
145. Matthew 11:30.
146. I John 4:16.
147. Bellevue in Washington County, Missouri; see the note above.
148. Cf. Hebrews 4:12, Revelation 1:16.
149. On Methodist quarterly meetings in this period, see Lester Ruth, *A Little Heaven Below: Worship at Early Methodist Quarterly Meetings* (Nashville: Kingswood Books, 2000).
150. Stevenson refers here to the great New Madrid earthquakes of 1811-1812, which began on December 16, 1811. Aftershocks continued for months afterwards.
151. Acts 16:29.
152. II Corinthians 5:1.
153. Stevenson's sense that the New Madrid earthquakes led to sincere repentance seems to echo Wesley's claims about the 1757 Lisbon earthquake: John Wesley, *Serious Thoughts occasioned by the late Earthquake at Lisbon*; in Thomas Jackson, ed., *The Works of the Reverend John Wesley, A.M.* (14 vols.; London: Wesleyan Conference Office, 1873), 11:1-13.

Although Stevenson may not have had direct access to the *Serious Thoughts*, John Wesley had written about the *Serious Thoughts* in his *Journal* for 26 November 1755, which was widely available: in W. Reginald Ward and Richard P. Heitzenrater, eds., *Journal and Diaries* (Bicentennial Edition of the *Works of John Wesley*; Nashville: Abingdon Press, 1988-2003), 21:35.

154. Walter Vernon pointed out a discrepancy in the dates from this point, hence the ambiguity in the section headings I have given. Vernon suggested that each of the dates Stevenson gave from this point on were a year earlier than the actual dates: cf. the first note on the introduction above and Vernon, "Beginnings of Methodism in Arkansas," *The Arkansas Historical Quarterly* 31:4 (Winter 1972), 358, n. 6.
155. Bellevue in Washington County, Missouri; see the notes above.
156. John 1:29.
157. An indication that 1841 was the year in which Stevenson composed hisn*Autobiography*; cf. the comments in the editor's introduction above.
158. Terre Noir.
159. Vernon noted that at this time, "Any Methodist preaching west of the Mississippi River would at that time be the responsibility of the Illinois District (not Conference) of the Tennessee Conference" (Vernon, "Beginnings of Methodism in Arkansas," 360, n. 8). A new conference was established in the next year that included a Missouri District that became an annual conference in 1816.
160. A verse from a hymn by Charles Wesley that appeared in his second series of *Funeral Hymns* (Bristol: W. Pine, 1769 [originally published in 1759]), 8. Presumably the hymn had been included in one of the American collections of hymns, though it did not appear in the 1780 *Collection of Hymns for the Use of the People Called Methodists*.
161. Probably 1815; see the notes above.
162. Vernon notes at this point that this event occurred in 1815 according to the published minutes of the Tennessee Annual Conference, which met in Lebanon, Tennessee, on October 15, 1815; hence Vernon's suggestion that the year of these events was 1815 rather than 1814.
163. Bellevue in Washington County, Missouri; see the notes above.
164. Stevenson is correct in representing Texas as a "province": it was organized as a province of New Spain from 1722; cf. Donald E. Chipman, "Spanish Texas," *Handbook of Texas Online* (http://www.tshaonline.org/handbook/online/articles/nps01), accessed March 26, 2015. Uploaded on June 15, 2010. Modified on November 25, 2013. Published by the Texas State Historical

Association. Pecan Point is on the Red River near the confluence of Pecan Bayou, in northern Red River County, Texas. This marks the first Protestant preaching in the area that is now the state of Texas; cf. Rex W. Strickland, "PECAN POINT, TX," *Handbook of Texas Online* (http://www.tshaonline.org/handbook/ online/articles/hrp20), accessed March 26, 2015; uploaded on June 15, 2010; published by the Texas State Historical Association. Walter N. Vernon points out that some of the settlers at Pecan Point had come from the same area of Tennessee (Smith County) where Stevenson had settled in and immediately after 1800: Vernon, *William Stevenson*, 38-42.

165. Vernon believed that this is a reference to Henry Stephens (sic), who was not related to Stevenson.
166. Mound Prairie, where Stevenson settled with his family. Ozan and Mound Prairie are both located in present-day Hempstead County, Arkansas, in the southwestern corner of the state very near the Texas border.
167. Since Stevenson was born in 1768, this would make the year of his writing this 1841; cf. the reference to this year in the text above.
168. The concluding note is presumably by Dr. McTyeire, the editor of the *New Orleans Christian Advocate* who had written the introduction to the first section of the *Autobiography*.